Primary to Secondary School Transition Workbook
A Helpful Transition Workbook to aid students move smoothly from
Primary to Secondary School

CreateSpace Independent Publishing Company
4900 LaCross Road
North Charleston, SC 29406
United States of America
Telephone: 1 843-760-8000

Website: www.createspace.com

8916 Eustace Bernard Drive, Ph 5. La Horquetta, Trinidad & Tobago
(868)463-5513. positivemindsetinc@gmail.com

<u>Acknowledgements</u>

The author of this book would like to sincerely thank the Lord God Almighty for all what he has done in her life. In the process of compiling and collating the information for this book, I realized how true this gift of writing and organization is for me. The Lord has given me the power to believe in my passion and pursue my dreams. This would not have been possible without the faith I have in him.

To my family: I can barely find the words to express all the wisdom, love and support you all have given me over the years. You all are the best family one could ever ask for and for this I'm eternally grateful.

To my Tech Savy Cousin, Shireen Danell Bellot: What can I say? You are awesome! Thanks for your assistance in organizing this document. You are indeed blessed with an awesome skill. May the Lord continue to bless those fingers!

To my student, Amilia Joy Wilda Jones: Thanks for introducing me to the publishers. If it wasn't for our interaction this publication wouldn't have been possible. Thank you so much. God's blessings be upon your life and your future endeavours.

To all those who have over the years contributed to my overall development as a professional in the field of Education, I sincerely thank you: Patricia Ettienne, Joseph Ragoonanan, Lyn Marie Osborne, St. George East Colleagues, Caribbean Nazarene College, Rhoda George (Nehemiah Comprehensive School), Mr. Max Andrews, Nicole Wyse and Mr. Clyde Best. God's blessings be upon your lives as you continue to contribute to the lives of others in this field.

Introduction

Transitioning from primary to secondary school education involves a degree of apprehension for most students. They have to adapt to a more challenging school setting with different academic structures and expectations as well as changes in social interactions with teachers and peers.

Most students are able to cope and feel accustomed by the end of the first couple of weeks; however, some experience tremendous difficulties in adjusting to their new environment and lifestyle. Change in the school environment can make students anxious. Anxiety about lack of control of their environment can lead to them feeling panicky all of the time contributing to a knock-on effect on their performance. They may lash out at others or withdraw into themselves in a form of self-protection.

Secondary schools are places of change. This causes additional strain on the student who is also trying to cope with their underlying difficulties and now has more problems layered on top. This can result in a breakdown in the student's mechanisms for coping and is why we sometimes see secondary school being a crisis time, after the child has seemingly being able to cope in primary school.

This workbook is designed to help these students who are having issues with transition. The information is displayed through easy-to-use and understand worksheets as well as notations on various topics. The topics covered in this workbook include differences between primary and secondary school, school systems & personnel, organization at home & school, friendship, bullying & cyber bullying, study skills, learning styles and career development.

Wishing you all the best with your secondary school education and use the information to help you with a smooth and successful transition.

Table of Contents

Effective Study Skills

Test Taking Skills

Career Development

Transitioning to Secondary School

Name: _____

Primary School: _____

Secondary School: _____

WHO AM I?

My name is _____

I am _____ years old

I was born on _____ (date)

My zodiac sign is _____

I was born at _____
(place, town, hospital)
I am of _____ descent.

I am _____ in complexion.

My hair is _____ in colour.

I am _____ in/ft/cm tall.

My mother's name is _____

My father's name is _____

I have _____ brothers and _____ sisters.

I live with my _____

My address is _____

_____

The name of my primary school is _____

I am a _____ student.
(Hardworking, careless, industrious, troublesome, etc.)

Some of my skills/interests are _____

_____

When I grow up, I would like to be a _____

What do you want to achieve at the end of your first term at secondary school?

_____

NAME POEM

Use the letters of your first and/or last name to create an acrostic poem.
Be creative and think positively!!!

Importance of a Secondary School Education

Write a paragraph below on the Importance of attaining a Secondary/High School Education.

_____

_____

_____

_____

_____

_____

_____

_____

_____

_____

_____

_____

Bye Bye Primary School, Hello Secondary School.

Contents

Differences between Primary & Secondary School

My New Secondary School

My School Collage

What are you looking forward to?

What are you worried about?

Differences between Primary and Secondary School

Identify the differences you have observed between your primary school and your secondary school.

AREAS	PRIMARY SCHOOL	SECONDARY SCHOOL
Buildings		
Teachers		
Age groups		
Subjects		
Time		
Travelling		
Others		

My Secondary School

Find a photo of your secondary school and stick it here.

The name of the School is _____

The address is _____

_____

The motto is _____

_____

The telephone number is _____

The e-mail address is _____

The website address is _____

The name of the Principal is _____

The name of the Vice-Principal is _____

My School Collage

Create a collage using pictures of different areas or buildings found on your school compound.

What are you looking forward to?

Changing from one environment to another can be very scary and overwhelming, causing us undue stress and anxiety.

Use two different coloured highlighters, highlight the phrases that you are looking forward to in one colour; use a different colour for those you are worried about.

Making new friends	Learning a new timetable
Lunch Break	Waking up earlier in the mornings
Using a different uniform	Being on time
Finding the way around	Break times
Getting to school	Learning new subjects
Meeting others my own age	Taxing by older students
Being with friends	School rules
Doing Homework	Meeting my new Principal
Meeting my new teachers	Being able to do the work
Travelling to school daily	Going on field trips
Bullying	Joining clubs and societies
Being with older pupils	Getting changed for sport / PE

What are you worried about?

Think about something that worries you about moving to Secondary/High School.

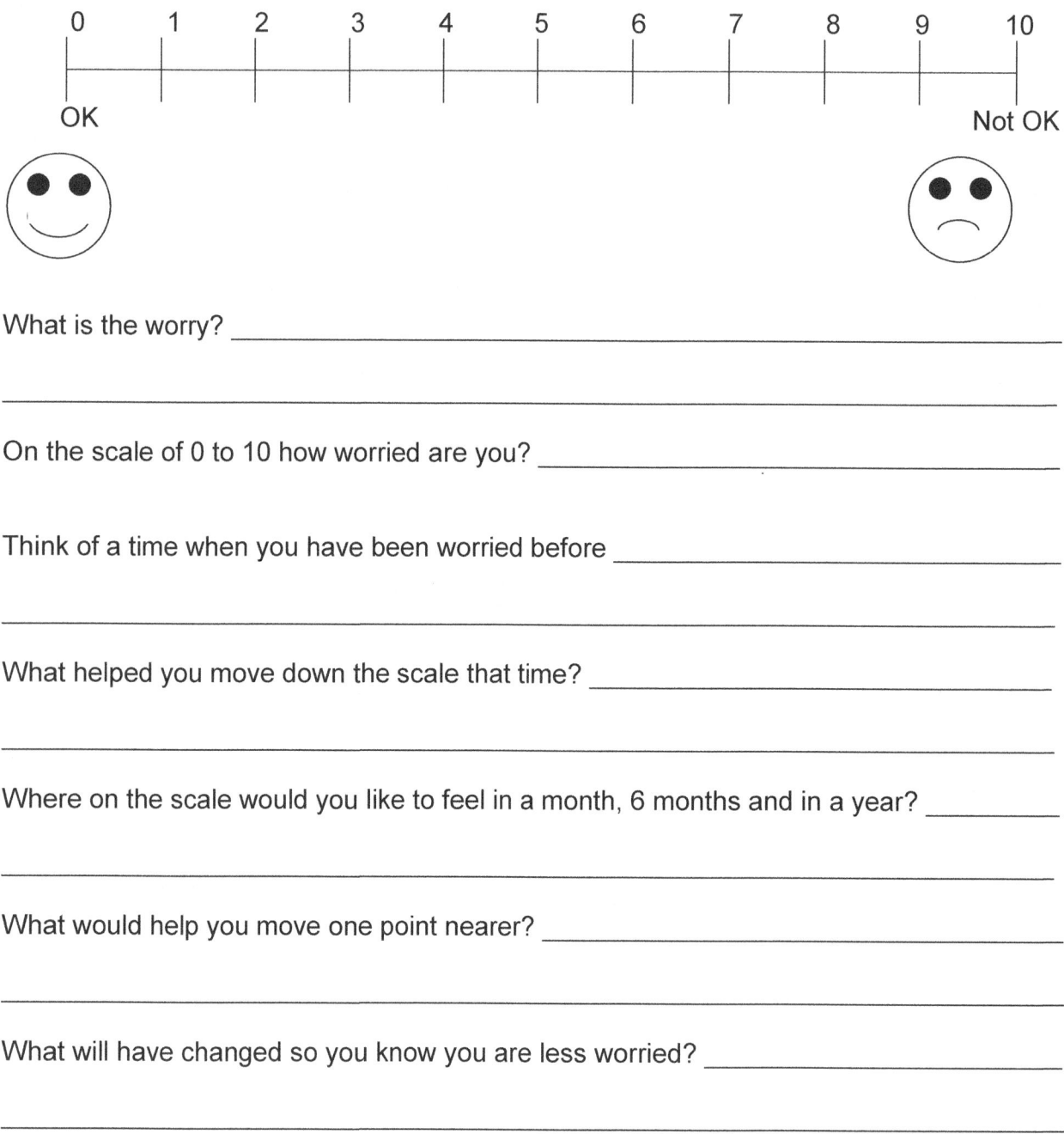

| 0 | 1 | 2 | 3 | 4 | 5 | 6 | 7 | 8 | 9 | 10 |

OK   Not OK

What is the worry? _____

_____

On the scale of 0 to 10 how worried are you? _____

Think of a time when you have been worried before _____

_____

What helped you move down the scale that time? _____

_____

Where on the scale would you like to feel in a month, 6 months and in a year? _____

_____

What would help you move one point nearer? _____

_____

What will have changed so you know you are less worried? _____

_____

My Secondary School Personnel & Systems

Contents

Finding Your Way Around

My Map of the Premises

School Staff

MY Guidance Counsellor

House Systems

Uniform Rules

My School Uniform

My P.E. / Sports Uniform

Finding your way around

It can be difficult to find your way around a new environment. Most importantly draw a map to help you remember where the various rooms are. Mark the rooms in different colours.

You may want to mark:

- Your Form Room
- The Library
- The Language Lab
- The Computer Lab
- The Art Room
- The Canteen/ Cafeteria
- The Student Toilets
- The Main Office
- Student's Entrance
- The Science Lab
- The AV Room
- The Hall/Auditorium
- The Parking Lot
- The Music Room

My Map of the Premises

School Staff

There are many teachers in a secondary school, not all of them will teach you, but may be important to you in a different way. As well as being a teacher they may have another job in school. The different names for these jobs are helpful to learn.

Written below are some of the jobs that adults in your secondary school may have.

Try and find out if there are adults in your secondary school who do this job, what they do and when you may see them.

The name of your form teacher _____

What do they do? _____

When may you see them? _____

The name of the 1st Form Dean _____

What do they do? _____

When may you see them? _____

The name of the Asst. Form Teacher _____

What do they do? _____

When may you see them? _____

Is there anyone else who might help you?

What is their name? _____

What do they do? _____

When may you see them? _____

The Guidance Counselor

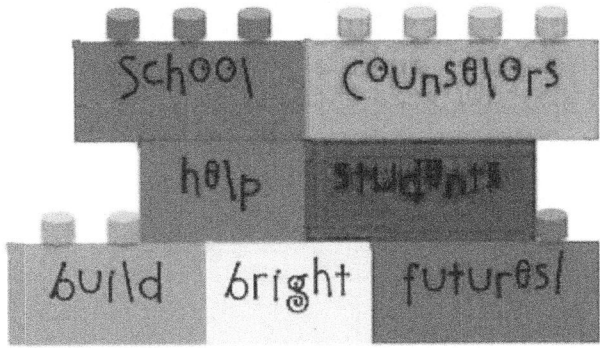

1. What is the name of your Guidance Counsellor/Officer? _____

2. Where is his/ her office located? _____

   _____

3. Give the meaning of the following words:

   a. Trauma _____

   b. Resiliency _____

   c. Advocate _____

   d. Punitive _____

4. List some of the main functions of the Guidance Counsellor.

   a. _____

   b. _____

   c. _____

   d. _____

   e. _____

5. How do you feel about having a Guidance Counsellor at your school?

   _____

   _____

House Systems

Some schools divide pupils into groups that include pupils from all year groups. These groups are often known as Houses. Often there are inter- house competitions to earn the most points. Points can often be earned for good work or behaviour. It is possible to lose points as well.

The name of your house is _____

The name of your Head of House is _____

What are some of the things you will earn points for?

1. _____

2. _____

3. _____

4. _____

I may lose points for:

1. _____

2. _____

3. _____

4. _____

School Uniform Rules

It is important to wear the right clothes when you start at Secondary School. Find out the school dress code and place a copy of the rules that apply to it.

My School Uniform

Picture of School Uniform

My P.E. / Sports Uniform

Picture of P.E. Uniform

Organisation at School

Contents

Bell Times

Morning Break

Lunch Break

My Canteen Weekly Budget

Healthy Eating

My Role as a Student

A Day in the Classroom

Bell Times

Write the times the bell rings for different intervals of the day.

Morning Break

At the end of a lesson you need to pack your bag, check to see if you have all your belongings and usually you have to leave the room in order to go to your next lesson. At some time in the morning you will usually have a longer break in which you have time for a snack and to meet up with your friends.

Give the times your first session in the morning starts and finishes. How long is your break?

Start [　　　] Finish [　　　] Length of break [　　　]

Where can I go and what can I do at morning break?

Place	What can I do?

What snacks can I buy at School?

1. _____

2. _____

3. _____

4. _____

Lunch Break

The lunch break is between morning and afternoon lessons. It is a time when you can socialize with your friends, go to a lunchtime activity, and eat your lunch.

State the time your lunch break starts and finishes. How long is your lunch break?

Start [   ]   Finish [   ]   Length of break [   ]

Where can I go and what can I do at lunchtime?

Most secondary Schools have a canteen or cafeteria on the compound or students can bring a packed lunch.

Make a list of some of the different types of food items you can buy in the canteen:

1. _____

2. _____

3. _____

4. _____

5. _____

REMEMBER you might need to bring in money if you decide to use the services of the canteen.

If you bring in a packed lunch you will need to find out

Where can you eat it? _____

What time do you eat it? _____

Can you buy a drink at school? _____

What sort of drinks or containers are you allowed to bring into school?

_____

_____

Lunch time activities- Some of the clubs and societies at the school hold their meetings at lunch time.

Make a list of the different activities you participate in during the lunch break.

1. _____

2. _____

3. _____

4. _____

5. _____

6. _____

7. _____

Places to go- there are often different places you can go during your lunch break

Place	What can you do?

My Canteen Weekly Budget

Find a menu from school with the prices. Make a budget of what you buy from the canteen and how much money you spend per week.

Day of the week	Food	Price
Monday		
Tuesday		
Wednesday		
Thursday		
Friday		
	Total for the week	

Discuss the menu you have chosen with your parents or Guidance Counselor.

- Have you chosen a variety of foods?

- Have you included fruit and vegetables in your choices?

- Are there at least 2 days that you have chosen healthy options?

Healthy Eating

Children at secondary school age are ready to learn about healthy food and activity. Breakfast is important. Some children are fussy or picky eaters, but snacking or grazing can be a good way to eat. School lunches and canteen food should be healthy and tasty.

Children need a wide variety of foods for a well-balanced diet. The amount of physical activity they have in a day will be an important part of how much they need to eat. When children are busy and active, snacking is important to keep energy levels high. A healthy morning snack at break and lunch are usually needed each day.

Breakfast is the most important meal of the day. A good night's sleep followed by food in the morning helps you to stay active and concentrate at school. It also means you are less likely to be too hungry during the morning and it can help with performance at school.

School lunches

Many schools have a canteen that offers a range of food choices. Most schools follow guidelines to encourage healthy food choices. The food you choose to eat might be high in cost and energy, but low in nutrients sometimes. An alternative is a packed lunch from home, which is a great way for you to learn about healthy food and to help with preparation.

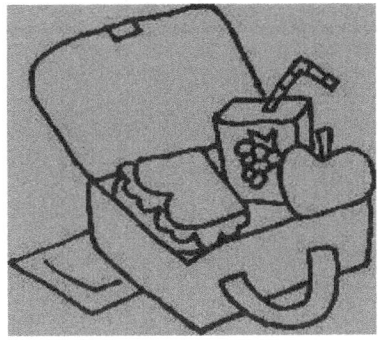

Lunch box suggestions include:

- Sandwiches or pita bread with cheese, lean meat, fish and salad
- Cheese slices, crackers with spread, and fresh or dried fruits
- Washed and cut up raw vegetables or fresh fruits
- Frozen water bottle or tetra pack of milk, particularly in hot weather.

School lunches – foods to limit

Highly processed, sugary, fatty and salty foods should only make up a very small part of your child's diet. Foods to limit in everyday school lunches include:

- Processed meats such as salami, ham, and pressed chicken
- Chips, sweet biscuits, and muesli bars and breakfast bars
- Fruit bars and fruit straps
- Juices and soft drinks.

Drinks

Suggestions include:

- Children should be encouraged to drink plain water.
- Sweet drinks such as cordials or fruit juice are not needed for a healthy diet and aren't recommended.
- A glass of milk (or a tub of yoghurt or slice of cheese) equals a serve of dairy food. Three serves are needed each day for calcium

My Role as a Student

Think about how you are expected to behave in Secondary School and the reasons for this. Include information on attending classes, working hard, performing well in tests, doing homework/assignments, producing work on time, cooperation and socializing with new people, and understanding the new environment etc.

_____

_____

_____

_____

_____

_____

_____

_____

_____

_____

_____

_____

_____

_____

_____

_____

A Day in the Classroom

1. Name three subjects on your timetable on Day 5.

   _____

   _____

   _____

2. Two ways I can participate in class are:

_____

3. What time is break? _____

4. What time does the school bell go for lunch? _____

5. How many class sessions/periods do you have per day on the timetable? _____

6. What is the name of your English Teacher?

   _____

7. What is the name of your favourite teacher?

   _____

Organisation at Home

Contents

Morning Routine

Getting to School Map

How will I get there?

Looking after Yourself

Personal Hygiene Questionnaire

Managing my Money

Parental Help

What do I need for School daily?

Morning Routine

Before leaving for School there are a lot of things to think about, starting from the night before.

Things to think about in the morning. Put them in the right order.

- Get dressed
- Check you have the correct books in your bag
- Check your timetable
- Take a bathe
- Check you have got your homework
- Clean your teeth
- Say "Goodbye"
- Check you have the enough money
- Wake up
- Eat your breakfast
- Leave for School

Any others?

- _____

- _____

Plan your morning routine with approximate times.

Time	What to do

Getting to School Map

Draw a map showing your journey from home to your secondary school.

How will I get there?

How will you get to School? _____

You might **walk** or **travel** sometimes, if you do then answer these questions:

Do I know the way?	
Will I have a friend to walk or travel with?	

You might go by **car** sometimes, if you do then answer these questions:

Will I go by car every day?	
Who will drive me?	
Will I get a lift home as well?	

You might go by **bus** or **maxi-taxi** sometimes, if you do then answer these questions:

Where is the bus/ Maxi stop	
What time is my bus/maxi to School?	
What number is the bus?	
Will I need money for the fare?	
What time is my bus/maxi from School?	

Answer these questions whether you will **walk**, **travel**, go by **car**, or **maxi-taxi**.

How long will my journey take?	
What time must I leave home?	
What time will I get home?	

Looking after Yourself

Keeping fit

- Get plenty of sleep
- Do some physical exercise at least once a week

Keeping clean

- Shower or bath and wash your hair regularly, probably at least 3 or 4 times a week. This can depend on how greasy your hair gets.
- Clean your teeth at least every morning and night
- Use deodorant every morning
- Change your underwear every day.

Looking smart

- Brush your hair every day and have your haircut regularly.
- Make sure your uniform is clean.
- Look in the mirror to check that you are tidy every day before you leave home.
- Clean your shoes regularly

Personal Hygiene Questionnaire

1. I wash my hands before eating
a) Always   b) Frequently   c) Sometimes   d) Never

2. I use soap to wash my hands
a) Always   b) Frequently   c) Sometimes   d) Never

3. I use antibacterial hand sanitizer
a) Always   b) Frequently   c) Sometimes   d) Never

4. I wash my hands after using the toilet
a) Always   b) Frequently   c) Sometimes   d) Never

5. I take a bath daily
 a) Always   b) Frequently   c) Sometimes   d) Never

6. I use a clean shirt for school everyday
a) Always   b) Frequently   c) Sometimes   d) Never

7. I wear clean and washed socks daily
 a) Always   b) Frequently   c) Sometimes   d) Never

8. I brush my teeth three times a day
a) Always   b) Frequently   c) Sometimes   d) Never

9. I cut my nails regularly
 a) Always   b) Frequently   c) Sometimes   d) Never

10. I take bath after playing
 a) Always   b) Frequently   c) Sometimes   d) Never

11. I wash my hair a minimum of once a week
 a) Always   b) Frequently   c) Sometimes   d) Never

12. I comb my hair tidily before going to school
 a) Always   b) Frequently   c) Sometimes   d) Never

Managing my Money

Now that you are at secondary school you will be responsible for managing your money on a daily and a weekly basis.

The amount of money I have each week is $____ . ____

Some of this money needs to be spent on a daily basis.

Items to be bought	Mon.	Tues.	Wed.	Thurs.	Fri.	Total
Snack						
Lunch						
Travel expenses						
Daily total						
					Weekly Total	

In addition to the money spent on a daily basis some money will need to be saved each week in order to buy other items who might need.

Items	Cost
Books	
Stationary	
Clothes	
Footwear	
Total cost	

I will try and save $ ___ . ____ every week.

Parental Help

Give this sheet to your Mum or Dad, or whoever helps you get ready for school

Ideas for helping your son/ daughter at home

The most important help you can give is continual encouragement and praise.

Talk

Encourage your son/ daughter
- To talk about School- likes/ dislikes, what they are good at, what they are worried about, issues affecting them, how they are coping with the transition…..
- To talk about books, films, hobbies etc.

Don't pressure them they will talk when they are ready.

Organisation

- Encourage them to make a large copy of their timetable
- Display it in a place where it is visible
- Refer to it to remind them what lessons they have each day
- Make lists of what they need each day
- Encourage them to pack their bag with everything they need for the next day
- Encourage them to check it against the list for that day
- Don't pack their bag for them
- Encourage them to get into a routine and do things in a similar sequence

Coursework

- Help plan out extended pieces of coursework over a period of days or weeks
- Check their homework diary/book each day
- Encourage them to have a set time to do their homework
- Encourage them to study every day.
- Help with homework
- Don't do their work for them
- Keep an eye on the time they spend on their work. Check they do not spend too long or too little time on each piece.

What do I need for school daily?

Things I need to bring every day

Every day you will need your writing equipment. Circle the equipment you need in your pencil case. Draw in anything else you need.

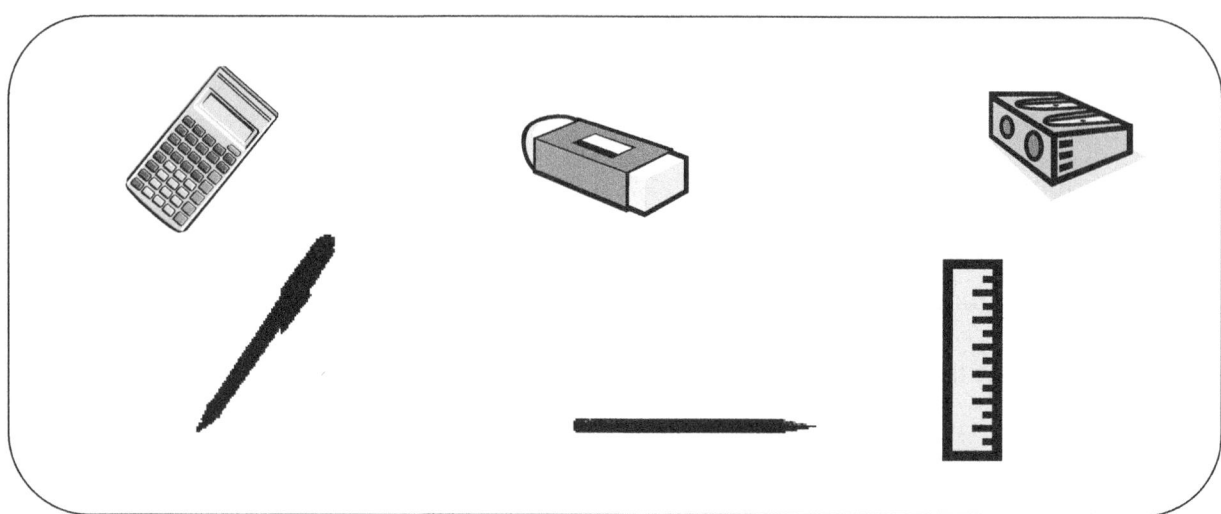

Some days you will need extra equipment. This will depend on the lessons you have that day. Look at your timetable and work out the additional equipment you need each day.

Day	Things I will need to bring
Monday	
Tuesday	
Wednesday	
Thursday	
Friday	

Friendship

Contents

My New Friend

Interview one of your classmates that you have met for the first time by asking him/her the list of questions below. After this exercise you will introduce your new friend to the rest of the class.

1. What is your name? _____

2. Where do you live? _____

3. What school did you attend before coming to this school? _____

4. How many brothers _____ and sisters _____ do you have?

5. What do you like most about school _____

6. What do you like least about school? _____

7. What is your favourite hobby? _____

8. What is your favourite book? _____

9. What is your favourite colour? _____

10. What is your favourite TV show? _____

11. What is your favourite food? _____

12. What is your favourite subject? _____

13. What is your favourite band/music? _____

14. What is your favourite sport? _____

15. What do you enjoy doing in your spare time?

_____

16. What career path are you interested in?

_____

Friendship Skills

Vocabulary Practice

Choose the right word to match the definitions.

> advocate   disagree   trust   respect   empathy   confidential
>
> compliment   advice   command   secret   support   apologise

1. _____   an opinion or recommendation you make about what someone should do

2. _____   to say you're sorry for something you said or did

3. _____   private or secret

4. _____   someone who defends and supports you

5. _____   to have a different opinion from someone

6. _____   to say something nice about someone

7. _____   information that's not meant to be shared with others

8. _____   to stand behind or encourage others

9. _____   understanding what someone feels

10. _____   to rely or have confidence in someone

11. _____   to hold someone in high esteem

12. _____   a direct order to do something

Being a Genuine Friend

Here are some positive things friends do for each other to keep their friendship strong.

- Always be there, even in silence

- **Acceptance.** Accept the person for who they are; without reservations

- **Forgiving.** Don't hold grudges over petty disagreements

- **Truthful**. Share the truth in your heart even though it might hurt sometimes.

- **Empathise**. Put yourself in your friend's situation to understand what they're going through.

- **Support**. You can show your support for your friends by just listening when they want to share.

- **Compliment**. Everyone likes to receive a compliment. Compliment your friend on a new hairstyle, a great score on a test, a smooth football move. Be specific and keep it simple. Choose the right moment to give the compliment.

- **Respect privacy.** Sharing secrets is a fun part of a friendship. It's hard to regain your friend's trust if you tell secrets you weren't supposed to share.

- **Encourage.** Use encouraging statements like, "You can do it".

When you wonder if you are being a good friend, ask yourself this question:

Am I treating my friend like I want my friend to treat me?

Building Friendships

Good friendships improve all aspects of your life, relieving stress, providing comfort and joy, strengthening your health, providing companionship, and preventing loneliness and isolation.

Whom to do you consider a friend?

_____

_____

_____

_____

What are some of the key characteristics of genuine friendships?

_____

_____

_____

_____

Why are friends important?

_____

_____

_____

_____

_____

_____

_____

Making new Friends

At Secondary school you will meet students for the first time. You will have the opportunity to interact with them and eventually make new friends. Sometimes, however, issues may exist whereby you may have difficulties meeting someone new.

It may help to act out meeting new people and use some of these suggestions.

- Smile when you say "**Hello**".

- Start the conversation by asking a question about what they are doing
  "**What are you doing?**" or "What **are you reading?**"

  or about something you have in common
  "**So how do you like this lesson?**"

- Introduce yourself
  "**By the way my name is _____, what's yours?**"

- Ask some other questions to find out about them. Suitable topics may be:

School: **What are you studying?**
             Who is your teacher?

Home: **Where do you live?**
             How do you get to School?

Interests: **What do you like doing?**
             What's your favourite TV programme?

Family: **Have you any brothers and sisters?**

- If they answer your question respond to some of the information they have told you. If you can, ask another question.
- Do not ask about
  "**That's my favourite lesson too. I enjoyed working on the computers. What did you like doing?**"

- Do not ask about sensitive topics. These are topics that could make the other person upset.

- Don't ask about something that makes the person look or sound different.

- Don't ask about any problems he or she may have.

Joining-In

Joining in conversation or a group activity can be scary. However, it is one way to make new friends. Try these strategies for joining in.

 **Watch and listen.** Observe what the group is doing. Listen to what the people are saying. Don't interrupt.

 Make a friendly comment or gesture. Nod your head and smile. Make comments like, "That's a good idea", or "That looks great".

 **Find something you have in common with the group.** Think about your own experiences. You could say, "I saw that movie", or " I have that game at home". Keep your comments short.

 **Ask to join the group.** Wait for a pause in the conversation. You could say, "Can I walk with you?" "Do you need any help?" or "Can I play?"

 **Accept 'no' for an answer.** Sometimes people don't want you to be part of the group. Don't argue or complain. Go and ask someone else.

Joining-in Situations

Here are some situations you might want to join in with. Try and plan what you may say or do. You could try acting these situations out.

1. You see three of your classmates playing football after school. You know one of them pretty well. You don't know the other two. You're quite good at being in goal.

   What could you do? _____

   What could you say? _____

2. You hear two classmates talking about the latest PlayStation game. You were playing on it last night.

   What could you do? _____

   What could you say? _____

3. Two classmates you know are gathered around a phone. A third classmate is calling a local radio station to try to win a contest. You think you may know the answer.

   What could you do? _____

   What could you say? _____

4. Four classmates are looking at a text message they have received from a friend. They are laughing. You're sitting at the same lunch table. You like sending text messages.

   What could you do? _____

   What could you say? _____

5. Two classmates are asking the teacher for permission to work on an art project during lunch hour. Art is your best subject and your project is already on display.

   What could you do? _____

   What could you say? _____

Being with Friends

Sometimes you have to think carefully about how you act with different people and whom you can share information with.

Getting it right

It is important to behave differently with different people.

Using the concentric circles sheet, work out who you would act in these ways with. You may choose more than one group of people.

1. Who would you hug?

2. Who would you use swear words with?

3. Who could you tell what to do?

4. Who can you argue with?

5. Who can you share your sweets with?

Make up your own: _____

_____

Sharing information about yourself

It is important to talk to people to share an event, achievement or tell them about a problem. Sometimes you have to be careful whom you talk to. Some people may tease you if you are not good friends or they may not keep the information to themselves and share it with others.

Who would you tell these things to? Use the concentric circles to decide who you would share the information with.

1. You still cuddle your teddy at night.

2. You fancy the girl or boy next door.

3. You have won a competition.

4. You have not done your homework.

5. You hate peas.

Sharing Information

Sometimes friends will tell you information. It can be OK to tell other people some bits of information. Other information you should tell no one, these are considered to be secrets.

It can be tempting to share secrets, but think:

- How will my friend feel if I share this secret?
- How will this affect our friendship?
- How would I feel if my friend shared a secret like this about me?

Who could you tell these things to?

1.   Your friend says that they like Sam.

2.   Your friend says their Dad is in jail.

3.   Your friend says they are going to watch a film tonight.

4.   Your friend says they hate wearing school uniform.

5.   Your friend says he smokes.

Make up your own: _____

_____

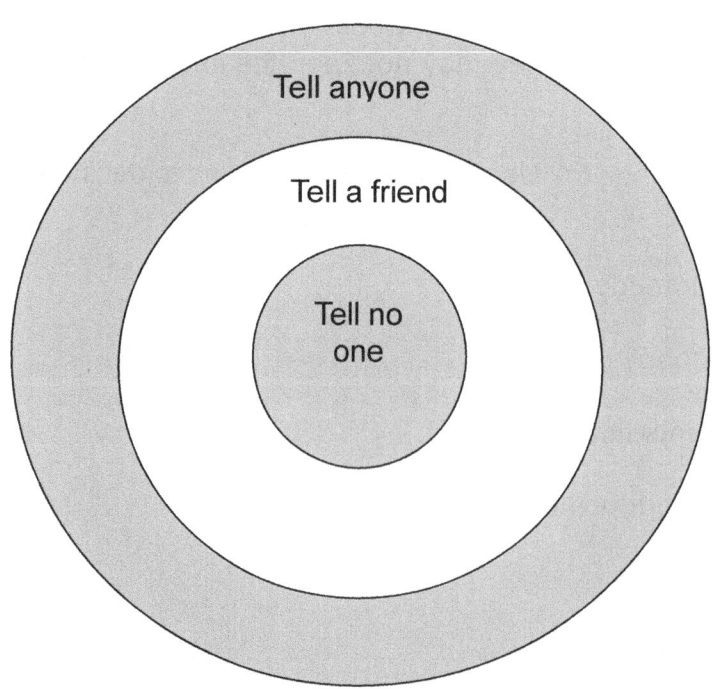

Awkward Situations

Contents

Teasing

What you need to know about teasing others

Facts about bullying

What to do about bullying

Bullying Worksheet

Cyber bullying

Cyber bullying Worksheet

Internet Safety Tips for Teens & Children

Fogging

Asking for help

Saying Sorry

Settling into Secondary School

Teasing

Teasing is to laugh at and criticize someone in a way that is either friendly and playful or cruel and unkind. Sometimes teasing is referred to as harassment and bullying, especially when the person is made to feel unhappy and hurt due to nasty teasing.

Students often tease others because they have learned that:

- People like to be entertained.

- People notice them if they are teasing.

- They feel powerful when others seem to be afraid of them (do you think that is really being powerful?)

- They like to be the centre of attention and they can't think how else to do it

- They can get away with it

- They don't have many ideas about how to get along with others.

- They think that it's OK to pick on some kids.

What you need to know about teasing others?

- When teasing upsets someone, everyone around feels uncomfortable.

- Teasing is not OK if it hurts people's feelings.

- Having people afraid of you is not as good as having friends.

- Being the centre of bad attention is not as great as being the centre of good attention.

- Picking on kids who are different in some way is never OK. That makes you a bully and no one likes bullies.

- If you tease others then no one will stick up for you when you are being teased.

- If you want to have friends then you need to learn how to be a friend.

- Everyone has a right to feel safe.

Maybe you thought teasing was cool because that's how you have been treated or are treated in some part of your life. If you are being teased then you need to read what you can do about it and ask for help to deal with it.

Facts about Bullying

Bullying:

- Is any behaviour by an individual or a group that deliberately harms another

- Can be physical or involve threats of physical harm.

- Can be name-calling or spoken teasing.

- Can be demanding money of things, or making someone do something they do not want to do.

- Can involve excluding someone (deliberately leaving someone out of an activity, ignoring them etc.)

- Is usually repeated over a period of time.

- Takes place when one person or group has more power than the person or group being bullied.

Bullying is not:

- An accidental bump or jostle, in the school corridor, for example.

- An argument with a friend.

- A friend being nasty over something specific.

- A one-off fight or argument.

Why do people bully?

- Very few people who are happy with themselves bully others

- Sometimes bullies have been bullied themselves - they are looking for someone to take their anger out on.

- Sometimes bullies are jealous.

- Bullying can make people feel strong, respected and powerful, but they often feel bad too.

What to do about Bullying

What can you do if you are bullied?

- Keep being positive; say positive things about yourself and other people.

- Be proud of who and what you are (we all belong to different groups and are all equally valuable).

- Don't keep it to yourself: Always tell someone- a teacher, a parent or another adult.

- Think about the consequences of the different ways you might deal with bullying.

- Some ways of dealing with it are:-

  - Ignoring it or staying relaxed, fogging (see next page)
  - Being assertive- using your body language, eye-contact, tone of voice, words you say.
  - Remember why people bully.

Six good reasons to tell:

- You have the right to live without the stress or fear of being bullied.

- Taking action is better than doing nothing.

- There is nothing embarrassing about being bullied- think how many people it happens to.

- It is braver to tell than to hide it.

- If you think there is something wrong with you, is it because the bullies have made you feel this way? This is a common effect of being bullied and **IT IS NOT TRUE**.

- Bullying does not say anything about **YOU**. It says a lot about the **BULLY**. (If you call me a hippopotamus does it mean that I am one?)

Bullying Worksheet

1. What is bullying?

_____

_____

2. Why is bullying harmful?

_____

_____

_____

3. What are some of the reasons why kids bully other kids?

_____

_____

_____

4. Describe an incident when you were bullied or someone you know was bullied.

_____

_____

_____

5. Who is a bystander?

_____

_____

6. What should you do if you are being bullied?

_____

_____

_____

7. What is the difference between bullying and teasing?

_____

_____

_____

Cyber Bullying

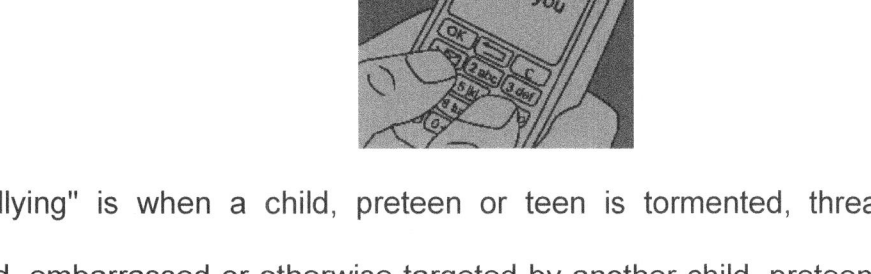

"Cyberbullying" is when a child, preteen or teen is tormented, threatened, harassed, humiliated, embarrassed or otherwise targeted by another child, preteen or teen using the Internet, interactive and digital technologies or mobile phones. It has to have a minor on both sides, or at least have been instigated by a minor against another minor.

The methods used are limited only by the child's imagination and access to technology, however, the cyberbully one moment may become the victim the next. The kids often change roles, going from victim to bully and back again.

There are two classifications of cyberbullying, direct attacks (messages sent to your kids directly) and cyberbullying by proxy (using others to help cyberbully the victim, either with or without the accomplice's knowledge).

Children have killed each other and committed suicide after having been involved in a cyberbullying incident.

Cyberbullying is usually not a onetime communication, unless it involves a death threat or a credible threat of serious bodily harm. Kids usually know it when they see it, while parents may be more worried about the lewd language used by the kids than the hurtful effect of rude and embarrassing posts.

Cyberbullying Worksheet

1. Define the term cyber bullying.

_____

_____

_____

2. Cyber bullying is also known as _____

3. Identify some differences between cyber bullying and traditional bullying?

_____

_____

_____

_____

4. Name five mediums used by cyber bullies.

_____

_____

_____

5. List five types of cyber bullying.

_____

_____

_____

6. What are some of the reasons why students cyber bully their peers?

_____

_____

_____

_____

_____

Internet Safety Tips for Children and Teens

- **Personal Information**. Don't give out personal information without your parents' permission. This means you should not share your last name, home address, school name, or telephone number. Remember, just because someone asks for information about you does not mean you have to tell them anything about yourself!

- **Screen Name**. When creating your screen name, do not include personal information like your last name or date of birth.

- **Passwords**. Don't share your password with anyone but your parents. When you use a public computer make sure you logout of the accounts you've accessed before leaving the terminal.

- **Photos**. Don't post photos or videos online without getting your parents' permission.

- **Online Friends**. Don't agree to meet an online friend unless you have your parents' permission. Unfortunately, sometimes people pretend to be people they aren't. Remember that not everything you read online is true.

- **Online Ads**. Don't buy anything online without talking to your parents first. Some ads may try to trick you by offering free things or telling you that you have won something as a way of collecting your personal information.

- **Downloading**. Talk to your parents before you open an email attachment or download software. Attachments sometimes contain viruses. Never open an attachment from someone you don't know.

- **Bullying**. Don't send or respond to mean or insulting messages. Tell your parents if you receive one. If something happens online that makes you feel uncomfortable, talk to your parents or to a teacher at school.

- **Social Networking**. Many social networking websites (e.g., Facebook, Twitter, and Snapchat) and blog hosting websites have minimum age requirements to sign up. These requirements are there to protect you!

- **Research**. Talk to your librarian, teacher or parent about safe and accurate websites for research. The public library offers lots of resources. If you use online information in a school project make sure you explain where you got the information.

Fogging

Fogging is a technique that you can use if you feel you are being bullied.

- Remind yourself that the bully has said this to many other people - what they say tells us more about the bully than about you.

- The bully wants to see your reaction - don't give them that satisfaction.

- Imagine a huge cloud of fog around you that swallows up insults so that they cannot affect you.

- Use a normal bored-sounding voice.

- Say something neutral:

    - "Yeah, whatever"
    - "If you say so"
    - "Well, you could be right"
    - "maybe"
    - "Ummm"
    - "Yes that's true, I do wear glasses"

- Make sure your body language, tone of voice and the words you use all give the same message:

    'I'm really not bothered by anything you say or do'

Stick with it. It might not work the first time.

Asking for Help

Sometimes at school things may be difficult or may go wrong. These things could be small:
- not knowing what the homework is
- not being able to find your way around

Or could be bigger:
- getting into trouble
- finding the work hard.

There are many people who could help you, but they won't know that you need help unless you tell them.

Friends Ask friends or other students if you don't know where to go. You can ask them what the homework was if you are not certain. They can also help to work out new situations like going to the cafeteria.

Teachers Ask your teachers if you don't know what to do in class or for homework. They will also be able to help you if you have forgotten something or don't know where to go.

People at home People at home will be able to help you plan and organise your equipment and homework. They will want to know if you have any problems. They will be able to help you work out the best person to ask if you have problems with work or may try and contact someone in school and ask them to help you.

Try and work out whom you would approach in these situations:

- You don't know where your next lesson is.

- You cannot read your homework notes.

- You have got into trouble for forgetting your course book several times.

- In the lesson you did not understand what the teacher wanted you to do.

- You have not got a pencil which is needed to complete your work.

REMEMBER TO ASK FOR HELP!

Saying Sorry

If you do break a school rule or behave in a way that upsets or hurts someone then you can show you are sorry by apologising. Sometimes this can be hard as it can be difficult to admit that you are wrong.

Here are some examples of times when you may need to say sorry.

When you forget something

- If you forget something, it is not a big problem. Everyone forgets things and it is always a good idea to say you are sorry.

- Imagine you have forgotten something. Practise saying the right words with a partner and then it will be easier when it does happen.

  For example:
  "I am sorry Sir / Miss. I'm not used to my timetable yet and I've forgotten to bring the right book. I will remember it for the next lesson."

When you make a mistake

- Mistakes can sometimes happen because you did not really understand what the teacher meant. Some things may be different from what you are used to and if you pretend that you understand when you don't the teacher will not know that you need help.

- Think up a situation in which you have not understood exactly what the teacher meant and discuss this with a partner. Take turns to explain to the teacher what has happened.

  For example:
  "I am sorry Sir / Miss, I have been listening, but I don't understand. Please could you tell me again?"

Settling into Secondary School
(How to solve the problems you might face)

Sometimes something can happen at school that makes you upset or anxious. A lot of people feel like this especially when they are starting somewhere new.

- **Keep calm.** Tell yourself, "I can solve this problem if I stay calm."

- **Decide what the problem is.**
  - Are you frustrated because you could not do something you wanted?
  - Are you upset because someone did something to you?
  - Are you worried because something has gone wrong?

- **Think about possible solutions.**

- **Think about the consequences.** What will happen if you try different solutions?

- **Pick the best solution.**

Talk with a friend about what you would do in each of these situations in school.

1. You haven't done your homework.

2. You have forgotten your student planner.

3. You are in a crowd going upstairs and you think someone pushed you.

4. You think you are lost.

5. You see someone being bullied.

6. You find someone crying in the corridor.

7. You've lost your purse/ wallet.

8. You see someone stealing money from someone's bag.

9. You find someone's purse.

10. You've ripped your trousers/ skirt.

Effective Study Skills

Contents

SQ3R Model

Difference between Studying & Doing Homework

Top Study Skills

Concentration

Tips to improve concentration

My Study Plan

My Study Strengths & Weaknesses

My Study Timetable

Study Environment Quiz

Learning Styles Inventory

SQ3R Reading Model

SQ3R is an acronym that stands for five steps that you should use when reading something that you want to remember. These five steps are: Survey! Question! Read! Recite! Review!

SURVEY
- the title, headings, and subheadings
- captions under pictures, charts, graphs or maps
- review questions or teacher-made study guides
- introductory and concluding paragraphs
- summary

QUESTION
- Turn the title, headings, and/or subheadings into questions
- Read questions at the end of the chapters or after each subheading
- Ask yourself,
  "What did my instructor say about this chapter or subject when it was assigned?"
- Ask yourself,
  "What do I already know about this subject?"
  Note: If it is helpful to you, write out these questions for consideration.

READ
- Look for answers to the questions you first raised
- Answer questions at the beginning or end of chapters or study guides
- Reread captions under pictures, graphs, etc.
- Note all the underlined, italicized, bold printed words or phrases
- Study graphic aids
- Reduce your speed for difficult passages
- Stop and reread parts which are not clear
- Read only a section at a time and recite after each section

RECITE
- Orally ask yourself questions about what you have just read, or summarize, in your own words, what you read
- Take notes from the text but write the information in your own words
- Underline or highlight important points you've just read

REVIEW
- Reread information/notes
- Discuss information/notes with someone else
- Schedule regular reviews of the material to keep it fresh in your mind

Applying the SQ3R Tool

Survey: Record important titles and subtitles from the reading selection.

_____

_____

_____

Question: Write "Who, What, Where, When, and Why" questions for the main topics in the selection.

_____

_____

_____

_____

_____

Read: As you read, write answers to your questions.

_____

_____

_____

_____

Recite: Record the key facts or terms necessary to know for this section.

_____

_____

_____

Review: Create a summary for the selection.

_____

_____

_____

Studying vs. Homework

The terms 'studying' and 'doing homework' are often used synonymously. However, there are some important differences in what they mean to you and how they should be approached.

1. *Homework* is material assigned by a teacher with a specific due date. It's about reinforcing knowledge and integrating key skills. Homework is a way for the student to begin learning at their own pace while involving their parents in the process if desired.

2. *Homework* often involves a lot of repetition. It typically repeats what you learned in school to help reinforce concepts. Repetitive exercises are often the best way to learn new vocabulary words or to utilize a new math idea.

3. *Studying* refers to time students set aside to go over key concepts from class and make sure their knowledge is complete. It is going over class material to ensure complete understanding. Studying is about learning on your own time, without the specific guidance of a teacher. Some teachers will provide students with study guides, but sometimes it is important that they also create their own study guides. The initiative involved in taking control of your own study patterns will help you become independent learners, preparing them for college and beyond.

4. *Studying* includes techniques such as re-reading unclear sections in the textbook, making flashcards, and taking notes on the textbook or on class notes. It involves a commitment to actually learning the key concepts that some homework assignments overlook. The easiest way to study for any type of test is to take notes on the textbook and notes from class. Flashcards are also useful for new vocabulary.

5. Encourage your child to study every day in short bursts, not just for the whole day before a test. If students commit to spending fifteen minutes going over the day's lesson in their hardest class, it will be a chance to truly understand the material. They will easily figure out what they understand and where they need assistance, which will allow you and their teacher to better help them learn. It will also tend to alleviate any pre-test stressing.

6. You can create your own study guides. These can be composed of lists of important dates, equations, concepts, or vocabulary. They may be more detailed, with key example problems and questions copied out of a textbook or class notes in a way that makes sense to you. You should not hesitate to ask your teachers what important concepts you should focus on when studying.

7. Prioritize. Do the most important things first! In the case of too much homework and a test, you may want to spend time completing homework instead of studying. The sense of accomplishment gained from completing a homework assignment isn't as clearly attained when studying, so you are tempted to invest your time on what you know you can finish. Help set a schedule that can include an hour of studying followed by a ten minute break. Set endpoints to make studying easier.

8. Studying goes above and beyond what the teacher provides for you. It necessitates self-starting. You should understand that what the teacher assigns, while good for reinforcing and expanding knowledge, is not enough for most students to fully prepare for tests.

Top Study Skills

Set goals.
- If you don't know what you want to achieve as a student, you won't know how to get there or if you've accomplished things.

Keep an appointment book or diary
- If you keep all your appointments, due dates, test dates in your head, you won't have any room left for the new information you are learning about in classes.

Know your learning style.
- Develop techniques and strategies for compensating for possible differences between your learning style and your teacher's teaching style.

Be an active reader.
- Be a text detective: ask your text good questions and it will yield good answers.

Participate in study groups.
- Share the load of reading and studying with other students – you will learn better by teaching them, and you will be exposed to ideas you didn't come up with on your own.

Take notes.
- Use the Cornell, outline, mapping or charting method to condense and synthesize reading, lectures and discussions.

Organize your study materials.
- If you organize your materials as you proceed through a course, you will retrieve information with greater ease later.

Draft papers.
- Never turn in the first draft of a paper – always leave time to re-work it before your teacher sees it.

Slow down on tests.
- Anxiety makes you skip over parts of questions. Read every word carefully.

Don't replace protein with caffeine.
- Protein and complex carbohydrates are an energy source that won't leave you jittery.

Concentration

Concentration is the ability to control your attention.

Causes of poor concentration

Distracting Noises

Your body condition (too tired or hungry)

Boredom

Day dreaming

Worrying

Dislike of the subject/ teacher

Wrong time of the day

TV, music, phone, games, food

Studying on a bed or on the floor

Overwhelming feeling about the task or assignment

Lack of commitment

Poor attention span

Lack of commitment

Not wanting to do the activity

Lack of sleep

Poor diet

Physical discomforts: headaches, growing pains, stomach aches or other physical aches and pains.

Tips to Improve Concentration

Promote a healthy diet— children can often have an increased intake of processed foods, saturated fats and sugary foods. Studies have shown that a diet rich in whole grains, fruits and veggies will help your child's brain functions. Also, studies have shown that children should avoid foods that have food colouring in them, as they may increase hyperactivity.

Set Routines— children need to have a routine (time for meals, school, homework), a ritual of things to do. Figure out a regular routine that will suit you and your child.

Limit the use of television and electronics—too much TV and computer games can prevent children from doing activities like, reading, doing homework, playing outside, and interacting with friends and with family.

Exercise more often—Both mental and physical exercise are very important to help your child concentrate better. For mental exercises, try playing board games that stimulate your child to think strategically and focus. Guessing games or even allowing them to help you cook by reading or following recipes. For physical exercise, it has been scientifically proven that children that do at least 30 minutes of exercise per day are more likely to do well in school, focus better and generally be more positive.

Support your child—Be there to support your child when they come home from school with homework, sit down and help them as they do their homework. Help them adopt an intention or willingness to study and learn. Help them understand their learning style and what time of day to study best. In addition, help them set clear and realistic goals.

Be honest and open with your child—Your children pick up on everything whether you believe they do or not. If something is going on within the family, talk to your child about his or her feelings. Try to exclude them from such distractions.

My Study Plan

Before study:

_____

_____

_____

During study:

_____

_____

_____

After study:

_____

_____

_____

Where I study:

_____

_____

_____

With whom I study:

_____

_____

_____

Diet & Exercise:

_____

_____

_____

My Study Strengths & Weaknesses

My study strengths are:

_____

_____

_____

_____

My study weaknesses are:

_____

_____

_____

Tips to help me combat my weaknesses

_____

_____

_____

_____

_____

My Study Timetable

This is the time table that I will be using after school each day and on weekends. I have to ensure that I balance my study time with recreation time including eating right, sleeping well and exercising regularly. I promise to follow this plan and make the best use of the education that has been afforded me.

Time	Monday	Tuesday	Wednesday	Thursday	Friday	Saturday	Sunday

My Study Environment Quiz

Read each of the following statements and mark them as either True (T) or False (F). Be sure to respond honestly. This will help you assess your own study habits.

1._____ I set aside time each day to study.

2._____ I don't usually study and watch TV at the same time.

3._____ I do my homework at a table or a desk with a bright light.

4._____ While I am doing my homework, I don't usually call or chat online

5._____ I have a dictionary to look up unfamiliar words.

6._____ When I sit down to work, I don't get up every few minutes.

7._____ When I need to work on a project, I know where to find the supplies I need.

8._____ I have a place where I keep my homework each night so that I remember to bring it to school.

9. My biggest obstacle to a positive study environment is

_____

_____

LEARNING STYLES INVENTORY

DIRECTIONS: To gain a better understanding of yourself as a learner, you need to evaluate the way you prefer to learn or process information. By doing so, you will be able to develop strategies which will enhance your learning potential. The following evaluation is a short, quick way of assessing your learning style(s).

		Often	Sometimes	Seldom
1	I can remember more about a subject through the lecture method with information, explanation, and discussion.			
2	I prefer information to be written on the chalkboard, with the use of visual aids and assignment readings.			
3	I like to write things down or to take notes for visual review.			
4	I prefer to use posters, models, or actual practice and some activities in class.			
5	I require explanations of diagrams, graphs, or visual directions.			
6	I enjoy working with my hands or making things.			
7	I am skillful with and enjoy developing and making graphs and charts.			
8	I can tell if sounds match when presented with pairs of sounds.			
9	I remember best by writing things down several times.			
10	I can understand and follow directions on maps.			
11	I do better at academic subjects by listening to lectures and tapes.			
12	I play with coins or keys in pockets.			
13	I learn to spell better by repeating the words out loud than by writing the words on paper.			
14	I can better understand a news article by reading about it in the paper than by listening to the radio.			
15	I chew gum or snack during studies.			
16	I feel the best way to remember is to picture it in your head.			
17	I learn spelling by "finger spelling," (drawing the letters with a finger).			
18	I would rather listen to a good lecture or speech than read about it.			
19	I am good at working and solving jigsaw puzzles and mazes.			
20	I grip objects in my hands during learning periods.			
21	I prefer listening to the news on the radio rather than reading about it in the newspaper.			
22	I obtain information on an interesting subject by reading relevant materials.			
23	I feel very comfortable touching others, hugging, handshaking, etc.			
24	I follow spoken directions better than written ones.			

LEARNING STYLES INVENTORY
SCORING PROCEDURES

Place the point value on the line next to the corresponding item.

OFTEN = 5   /   SOMETIMES = 3   /   SELDOM = 1

NUMBER	POINTS
2	
3	
7	
10	
14	
16	
19	
22	
Total Visual	

NUMBER	POINTS
1	
5	
8	
11	
13	
18	
21	
24	
Total Auditory	

NUMBER	POINTS
4	
6	
9	
12	
15	
17	
20	
23	
Total Tactile	

VISUAL LEARNINGS: Visual learners relate most effectively to written information, notes, diagrams and pictures. Typically they will be unhappy with a presentation where they are unable to take detailed notes – to an extent, information does not exist for a visual learner unless it has been seen written down. This is why some visual learners take notes even when they have printed course notes on the desk in front of them. Visual learners will tend to be most effective in written communication, symbol manipulation, etc. Visual learners should look at all study materials. They should use charts, maps, filmstrips, notes, and flashcards. Visual learners should practice visualizing or picturing words / concepts in their heads. Visual learners should write down everything for frequent and quick visual reference. **Visual learners make up around 65% of the population.**

AUDITORY LEARNERS: Auditory learners relate most effectively to the spoken word. They will tend to listen to a lecture, and then take notes afterwards, or rely on printed notes. Often information written down will have little meaning until it has been heard – it may help auditory learners to read written information aloud. Auditory learners may be sophisticated speakers, and may specialize effectively in subjects like law or politics. Auditory learners may want to use tapes. Taped lectures may help fill in the gaps in the student's notes. Auditory learners should sit in front of the classroom where they can hear well. Auditory learners should do reading assignments out loud, or recite summaries of written materials. **Auditory learners make up about 30% of the population.**

TACTILE LEARNERS: Tactile learners learn effectively through touch, movement and space. They learn skills by imitation and practice. Tactile learners often work slowly because information is normally not presented in a style that suits their learning methods. Tactile learners may also benefit from typing notes, and/or acting out (role playing) different situations. For example, tactile learners might pretend they are different parts of the cell and actually move about the classroom when studying cell structure. **Tactile learners make up about 5% of the population.**

TEST TAKING SKILLS

Content

Reducing Test Taking Anxiety

Test Preparation Tips

Test Taking Tips

Post Test Tips

Cramming Techniques for Exams

Test Taking Tips for Parents

Reducing Test Taking Anxiety

Test anxiety is when a student worries about doing well on a test. This can become a major hindrance on test performance and cause extreme nervousness, difficulty concentrating, racing thoughts and memory lapses among other symptoms. You can reduce test taking anxiety by:

- Being well prepared for the test.

- Spacing out your studying over a few days/weeks and continually review class notes.

- Maintaining a positive attitude while preparing for the test and during the test.

- Getting a good night's sleep before the test.

- Showing up to class early so you won't have to worry about being late.

- Staying relaxed, if you begin to get nervous take a few deep breaths slowly to relax yourself.

- Reading the directions slowly and carefully.

- Asking the teacher to explain the directions that you don't understand on the test

- Skimming through the test so that you have a good idea how to pace yourself.

- Writing down important formulas, facts, definitions and/or keywords in the margin first so you won't worry about forgetting them.

- Doing the simple questions first to help build up your confidence for the harder questions.

- Not worrying about how fast other people finish their test; just concentrate on your own test.

- Focusing on the question at hand. Don't let your mind wander on other things.

- Seeking help from your school counsellor if you're still experiencing extreme test anxiety after following these tips.

Test Preparation Tips

- Preparation for your first test should begin on the first day of class; this includes paying attention during class, taking good notes, studying, completing homework assignments and reviewing study materials on a regular basis.

- Budget your time, make sure you have sufficient time to study so that you are well prepared for the test.

- Pay attention to hints that the teacher may give about the test. Take notes and ask questions about items you may be confused about.

- Ask the teacher to specify the areas that will be emphasized on the test.

- Eat before a test. Having food in your stomach will give you energy and help you focus.

- Put the main ideas/information/formulas onto a sheet that can be quickly reviewed many times, this makes it easier to retain the key concepts that will be on the test.

- Show up early for your test/exams start.

- Set your alarm and have a backup alarm set as well.

Test Taking Tips

- Bring at least two pens/pencils with good erasers, a calculator with enough batteries and any other resources that your instructor allows you to.
- Bring a watch to the test so that you can better pace yourself.
- Keep a positive attitude throughout the whole test and try to stay relaxed. If you start to feel nervous take a few deep breaths to relax.
- Keep your eyes on your own paper, you don't want to appear to be cheating and cause unnecessary trouble for yourself.
- When you first receive your test, do a quick survey of the entire test so that you know how to efficiently budget your time.
- Do the easiest problems first. Don't stay on a problem that you are stuck on, especially when time is a factor.
- Do the problems that have the greatest point values first.
- Pace yourself, don't rush. Read the entire question and pay attention to the details.
- Ask the instructor for clarification if you don't understand what they are asking for on the test.
- Write legibly. If the grader can't read what you wrote, they'll most likely mark it wrong.
- Always read the whole question carefully. Don't make assumptions about what the question might be.
- If you don't know an answer, skip it. Go on with the rest of the test and come back to it later. Other parts of the test may have some information that will help you out with that question.
- Don't worry if others finish before you. Focus on the test in front of you.
- If you have time left when you are finished, look over your test. Make sure that you have answered all the questions. Only change an answer if you misread or misinterpreted the question because the first answer that you put is usually the correct one. Watch out for careless mistakes and proofread your essay and/or short answer questions.
- Double check to make sure that you put your first and last name on the test.

Post Test Tips

- When you get your test back look it over and make sure that there are no grading mistakes.

- Look over the test and make sure that you understand your mistakes. If you don't know the answer to a question, look it up, ask a classmate or ask the teacher.

- If the teacher reviews the test in class, be sure to take notes on what the teacher wanted for an answer on the questions/problems that you got wrong.

- If you aren't satisfied with your grade, go to your instructor and see if there's a make-up exam or any extra credit you can do.

- Save the test as study material for future tests.

Cramming Techniques for Exams

Cramming for exams should be avoided at all costs. You should only cram for an exam as a last resort. It's hard to take in and retain a large amount of information in a short period of time. Some of the tips on studying and preparing for a test may overlap with the cramming techniques below.

- Eat some food to give you energy to study but avoid consuming excess sugar which will make you hyper and will make it more difficult to study.

- An apple does a better job at keeping you focused and awake than caffeine.

- Find a well-lit place with no distractions around to study but don't get too comfortable or you may fall asleep.

- Keep a positive attitude, it is easier to study when you are relaxed than when you are stressed out.

- Since your time is limited, you have to choose what you study. Don't attempt to learn everything, focus on things that will get you the most points on the exam.

- Focus on the main ideas and learn key formulas. Skip the details for now and only come back to them if you see that you have time after you have learned the key points.

- Write down the key ideas/formulas on a sheet of paper and keep on studying from that sheet, repetition is important.

- Highlight the important points in your notes, and text and focus on that.

- Read the chapter summaries (they usually do a good job at summarizing the important points). If there're no chapter summaries then skim through the text and write down key ideas.

- Study from past tests, review questions, homework & review sheets.

- Take at least one five minute break an hour so that you can gather your thoughts and let your brain relax.

- If time permits, try to get at least 3 hours of sleep (one sleep cycle) before the exam so that you don't fall asleep when taking your exam. Don't forget to set your alarm!

Test Taking Tips for Parents

- Make sure that your child does all their homework and reading assignments, this will help make sure your child is prepared for the test.

- Encourage your child to space out their studying and homework assignments so that they won't be forced to cram on the night before the test.

- If you are anxious about your child's test, it's ok but try to keep cool around your child, you don't want them to get anxious about their tests too.

- Encourage your child to do well but don't pressure him/her. You may stress him/her out. It is important for your child to stay relaxed for the test.

- Keep a positive attitude about tests.

- Provide a quiet, well lighted area with little distractions to help your child study efficiently.

- Mark down test days on your calendar so you and your child are both aware of testing dates.

- Make sure that your child gets enough sleep on the night before the test.

- Ensure that your child eats a healthy breakfast and avoid heavy foods that may make him/her groggy and avoid high sugar foods that may make him/her hyper.

- Make sure that your child gets up early enough so that he/she will be on time to school.

- Let your child relax for a few hours before bedtime, it can be stressful for a child to study all night.

- Talking about the test with your child can relieve stress about test taking.

- If your child is struggling on their tests, talk to them about it and meet with their teacher to find out the best way to help your child.

- Praise/reward your child when they do well on a test or for their hard work preparing for a test.

- Review the test with your child after they have taken it and go over any mistakes they have made and make sure that they understand what they did wrong and how they can improve for the next test.

Career Development

Content

Cruise Into Your Future

Career Development Map

Holland's Personality Types

16 Career Clusters

Definition of terms

Developing my Career Plan

My Career Interest

Cruise Into Your Future

Life is a journey filled with many twists and turns. While the journey can be exciting, it's a good idea to know where you are going so you can decide how to get there. That's what career development is all about. Getting the knowledge and skills you need to make more informed career decisions. Right now is an excellent time to develop skills that will help you manage your career throughout life. The following steps can get you started down a pathway for a lifetime of choices:

1. WHO ARE YOU?

A. Learn about your interests, what you like and dislike.
B. Study your personality and how it fits into different work environments.
C. Your values can also help to determine where you work and how you want to work.
D. Don't forget skills; ones you develop throughout school and those you continue to develop past high school.

2. WHERE ARE YOU GOING?

A. Learn about the economy, the labour market, and the impact of technology on jobs.
B. Explore occupations and how they connect to your interests and abilities.
C. Learn about education and training options past high school and how financial aid can be used to finance your education/training.

3. HOW WILL YOU GET THERE?

A. Identify the careers and career cluster area that you find most interesting.
B. Set short and long-term goals.
C. Select required and elective high school courses.

Career Development Map

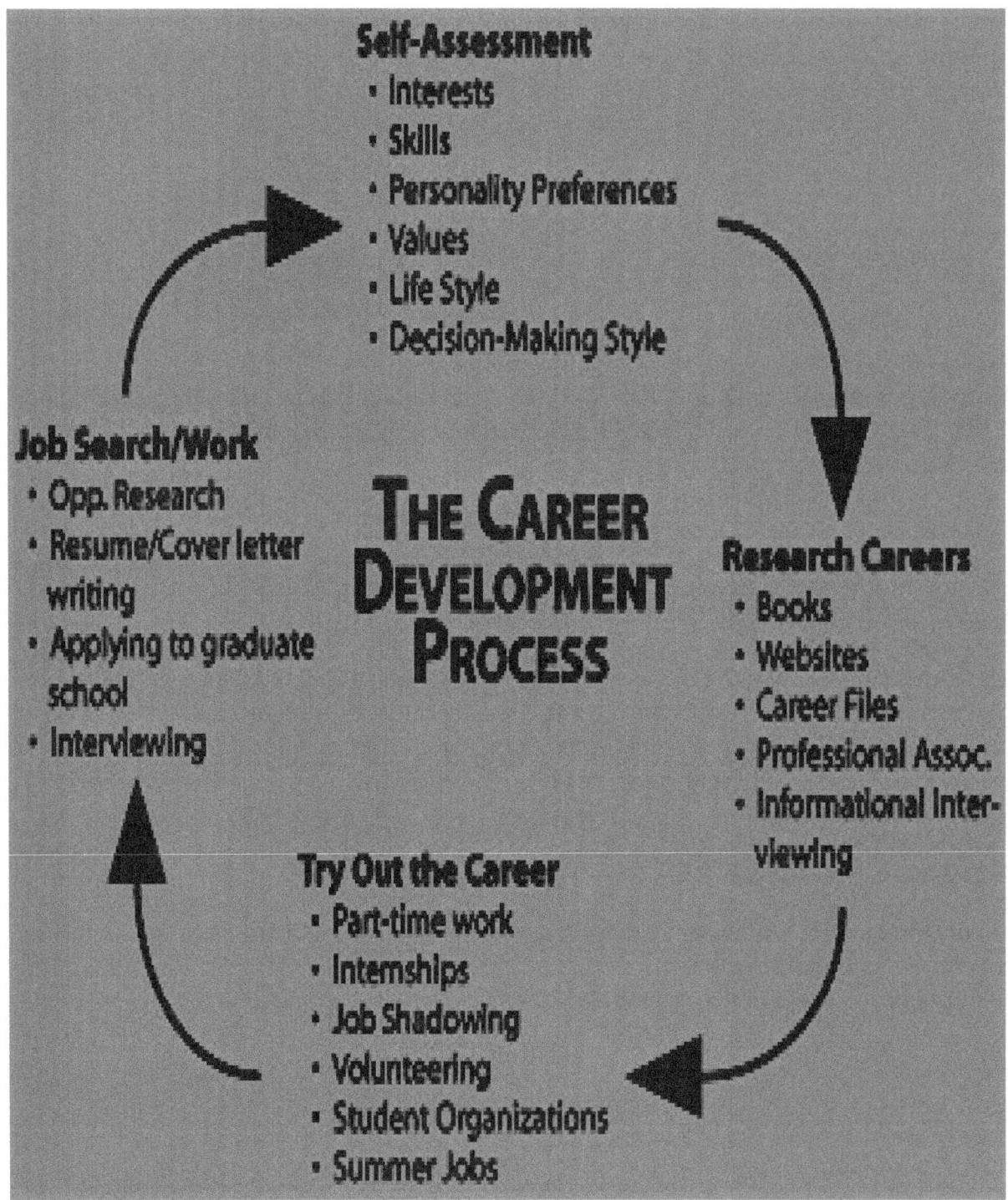

Self-Assessment
- Interests
- Skills
- Personality Preferences
- Values
- Life Style
- Decision-Making Style

THE CAREER DEVELOPMENT PROCESS

Job Search/Work
- Opp. Research
- Resume/Cover letter writing
- Applying to graduate school
- Interviewing

Research Careers
- Books
- Websites
- Career Files
- Professional Assoc.
- Informational Interviewing

Try Out the Career
- Part-time work
- Internships
- Job Shadowing
- Volunteering
- Student Organizations
- Summer Jobs

Holland's Six Personality Types

According to John Holland's theory, most people are one of six personality types

Realistic

- Likes to work with animals, tools, or machines; generally avoids social activities like teaching, healing, and informing others;
- Has good skills in working with tools, mechanical or electrical drawings, machines, or plants and animals;
- Values practical things you can see, touch, and use like plants and animals, tools, equipment, or machines; and
- Sees self as practical, mechanical, and realistic.

Investigative

- Likes to study and solve math or science problems; generally avoids leading, selling, or persuading people;
- Is good at understanding and solving science and math problems;
- Values science; and
- Sees self as precise, scientific, and intellectual.

Artistic

- Likes to do creative activities like art, drama, crafts, dance, music, or creative writing; generally avoids highly ordered or repetitive activities;
- Has good artistic abilities -- in creative writing, drama, crafts, music, or art;
- Values the creative arts -- like drama, music, art, or the works of creative writers; and
- Sees self as expressive, original, and independent.

Social

- Likes to do things to help people -- like, teaching, nursing, or giving first aid, providing information; generally avoids using machines, tools, or animals to achieve a goal;
- Is good at teaching, counselling, nursing, or giving information;
- Values helping people and solving social problems; and
- Sees self as helpful, friendly, and trustworthy.

Enterprising

- Likes to lead and persuade people, and to sell things and ideas; generally avoids activities that require careful observation and scientific, analytical thinking;
- Is good at leading people and selling things or ideas;
- Values success in politics, leadership, or business; and
- Sees self as energetic, ambitious, and sociable.

Conventional

- Likes to work with numbers, records, or machines in a set, orderly way; generally avoids ambiguous, unstructured activities
- Is good at working with written records and numbers in a systematic, orderly way;
- Values success in business; and
- Sees self as orderly, and good at following a set plan.

16 Career Clusters

Career clusters are groups of similar occupations and industries. There are 16 clusters which will help you learn all about all kinds of career possibilities, the knowledge and skills you'll need to succeed, and trends and technologies that are transforming the workplace.

As a Secondary student it will help you discover your interests and passions, and empower you to choose the educational pathway that can lead to success in high school, college and career.

- **Agriculture, Food, and Natural Resources**: This area refers to jobs that involve being outdoors and working with your hands. Examples of occupations within this area include animal trainer, groundskeeper, and greenhouse manager.

- **Architecture and Construction:** This area encompasses all the jobs that are involved in the building, maintenance, and operation of businesses and residential properties. Occupations within this area include architect, drafter, and electrician.

- **Arts, A/V Technology, and Communications**: Creative people who love using their talents to entertain and inform others are drawn to jobs in this career cluster. Examples of jobs within this area include journalist, commercial artist, and actor.

- **Business, Management, and Administration:** Entrepreneurial people who are highly organized and enjoy working with others often find business to be a suitable career area. Examples of jobs in this career cluster include accountant, administrative assistant, and human resources manager.

- **Education and Training:** If you're patient and enjoy helping others, working in the education field can be a rewarding experience. Potential job opportunities in this field include elementary school teacher, secondary school teacher, college professor, and corporate trainer.

- **Finance**: As you might expect, being successful in finance related careers requires strong mathematical ability and a solid attention to detail. Examples of careers in this cluster include loan officer, stock broker, and credit analyst.

- **Government and Public Administration**: Careers in government and public administration are varied, but all offer the satisfaction of knowing you're making a contribution to your community. Jobs in this area include solider, legislator, and Foreign Service officer.

- **Health Science**: Health science careers encompass all aspects of the medical field. Examples of career opportunities in this area include pharmacist, paramedic, and optometrist.

- **Hospitality and Tourism:** Hospitality and tourism is a rapidly growing industry with a great deal of room for advancement. Examples of careers within this cluster include chef, lodging manager, and food service manager.

-

-

- **Human Services:** The human services career cluster refers to jobs with the primary purpose of helping families meet basic human needs. Jobs in this area include social worker, psychologist, and substance abuse specialist.

- **Information Technology:** Jobs in information technology deal with computer hardware, software, and systems integration services. Potential job opportunities in this career cluster include positions such as web designer, network administrator, and technical support specialist.

- **Law, Public Safety, Corrections, and Security**: Protecting the well-being of the public at large is the goal of occupations in this area. Examples of jobs in this cluster include attorney, firefighter, and police officer.

- **Manufacturing:** People who work in manufacturing jobs use their strong mechanical abilities to create many different kinds of products. Examples of occupations in this area include sheet metal worker, millwright, and quality control technician.

- **Marketing, Sales, and Service:** This career cluster allows people to use their creativity and communications skills to meet a variety of business objectives. Some of the many job opportunities in this field include marketing director, customer service representative, and sales associate.

- **Science, Technology, Engineering, and Mathematics:** Careers in this area often involve cutting edge research into new technological developments. Jobs available include chemical engineer, oceanographer, and biotechnologist.

- **Transportation, Distribution, and Logistics**: Jobs in this cluster involve moving people, materials, and products by road, air, rail, and water. Examples of career opportunities include truck driver, pilot, and flight attendant.

Definition of Terms

Define the following terms:

Career:_____

_____

Job:_____

_____

Occupation:_____

_____

Profession:_____

_____

Skills:_____

_____

Interest:_____

_____

Values:_____

_____

Personality:_____

_____

Career goal: _____

_____

Developing my Career Plan

My Career goals:

_____

_____

_____

_____

My Interests:

_____

_____

_____

_____

My Values:

_____

_____

_____

_____

My Skills

_____

_____

_____

_____

My Career Interest

Identify three careers that you are interested in pursuing. (Illustrate using pictures)

Key Transition Difficulties

- ❖ Negotiating the way around school – student may get lost and this may result in being late for class
- ❖ Meeting new children with different personalities and temperament
- ❖ Meeting new teachers
- ❖ Learning about the rules of the school – explicit and implicit
- ❖ Learning new teachers' names and their expectations and styles of teaching
- ❖ Learning about the timetable and the appropriate books and tools required
- ❖ Understanding the timetable, especially the Day System
- ❖ Carrying equipment around all day – no central place to return to – therefore increasing the chances of losing equipment or having incorrect equipment for the next class
- ❖ Coping with change determined by others not themselves
- ❖ Independently organising work and managing timetable
- ❖ In PE and games coping with more complex activities such as changing in/out of PE kit
- ❖ At break times there is less supervision from teaching staff so the students are able to wander around on their own more (not seeking social interaction) or be more open to being bullied by others
- ❖ Coping with new topics students have not studied before.

Parents Role in Transition

- Help build your child's confidence. Settling in well is all about self-esteem. Children with high self-esteem are less likely to be bullied, or to bully, or belong to gangs. They are more likely to gather a wide circle of friends.

- Listen to their fears. Your child will be anxious and afraid about going to a new school. Take time to listen to the events of their day, especially any issues that they might be having.

- Remind your child that being a good friend, especially to shy and quiet children, is one way to make friends. Be encouraging if they want to invite friends home and suggest it if they don't.

- Show that you feel positive about their school and "talk it up" even if it was not your first choice. If you have high expectations, these will be sensed by your child.

- Have a trial run of the route, especially if they have to travel. On the other hand, if you are working and can't pick them up, they will have to know how to get home.

- Get up earlier during the last week of the holidays so that early starts for school aren't a shock to the system.

- Stick to the uniform code. Your child will feel more comfortable from day one.

- Make sure they have emergency money and credit on their mobile phone – if it's allowed in school.

- Think about any changes you might need to make at home so they have the time, space and energy for homework.

- Encourage them to join lunchtime or after-school clubs and societies. They are a great way to make friends and improve their confidence.

- Give your child a few weeks to settle in. If they are having any problems, social or educational, make an appointment to see their Principal or school counsellor.

Made in United States
North Haven, CT
04 April 2025

67562202R00057